Using the Expressive Arts with Children and Young People Who Have Experienced Trauma

This guide has been written to accompany the book *The Silent Selkie*, a children's story about trauma and offers gentle, creative ways for adults to work with children and young people who have faced adverse childhood experiences.

This guidebook:

- Explores the themes of the story and offers guidance to the adult as they use expressive arts to give the child or young person a way to process their emotional experiences.
- Supports trusted adults around the child or young person to understand trauma, its impact and how to respond appropriately and sensitively to the child.
- Provides techniques, exercises, and activities to encourage healthy creative expression and to help the child or young person to understand trauma, its impact and what can help.

Using this guide may be a first step on a young person's journey towards healing, making this an ideal tool for adults working with children who have experienced trauma, such as SENDCos, teachers, teaching assistants and family support workers.

Juliette Ttofa is a specialist educational psychologist and child therapist with a long-standing interest in the complex issues surrounding trauma, attachment needs and emotional resilience.

T0372207

'An excellent contribution and resource for those working with the troubled child. This hauntingly beautiful story will appeal to many children who have suffered from a variety of traumatic experiences. It will help them to make sense of their situation and reassure them that they are not alone in their inner pain. The guidebook will provide understanding of adverse childhood experiences and offer valuable skills and ideas for the adult who wishes to work alongside such children in a creative way.'

Eunice Stagg, *President – Association for Sandplay Therapy. BACP Snr Accredited Counsellor, Essex, UK*

Using the Expressive Arts with Children and Young People Who Have Experienced Trauma

A Practical Guide

Juliette Ttofa

Illustrated by Paul Greenhouse

Routledge
Taylor & Francis Group

LONDON AND NEW YORK

Cover image @ Paul Greenhouse

First published 2022
by Routledge
4 Park Square, Milton Park, Abingdon, Oxon OX14 4RN

and by Routledge
605 Third Avenue, New York, NY 10158

Routledge is an imprint of the Taylor & Francis Group, an informa business

British Library Cataloguing-in-Publication Data
A catalogue record for this book is available from the British Library

Library of Congress Cataloging-in-Publication Data
A catalog record for this book has been requested

ISBN: 978-0-367-63947-1 (pbk)
ISBN: 978-1-003-12144-2 (ebk)

DOI: 10.4324/9781003121442

Typeset in Calibri
by Apex CoVantage, LLC

Contents

Contents

Introduction

This guide has been written to accompany the book *The Silent Selkie*, which is a children's story about trauma.

The Silent Selkie describes a character who is unable to communicate in words and whose only way of communicating is through the weather, which leads to disastrous consequences not only for the Selkie, but also for everyone around her.

But behind her golden scales, the Selkie hides a secret wound that even she is unaware of, and it is only when the Selkie's skin becomes uncovered by the force of the sea that she remembers the terrible story of what caused her hurt, long ago. Only then can the Selkie awaken to come to terms with her wound and begin a journey of healing that will bring her face-to-face with what she has needed all along.

Without being specific about the detail of a traumatic event, *The Silent Selkie* deals with the effects of trauma on a young person – including hypersensitivity and emotional reactivity. The story uses the metaphor of trauma as a 'hidden wound', which is an emotional or psychological pain that needs both acknowledgement and expression, within the context of a safe, supportive environment, in which to begin to heal.

This guide to *Using the Expressive Arts with Children or Young People who Have Experienced Trauma* offers gentle, creative ways for adults to work with children and young people who have a background of trauma. It explores the themes of the story and offers guidance to the adult as they use expressive arts to give the child or young person a way to process their emotional experiences. The key aims of this guide and the storybook are:

- To support trusted adults around the child or young person to understand trauma, its impact, and how to respond appropriately and sensitively to the child.

- To present gentle ways for trusted adults to use creative expression to help children to begin to process the untold stories of their past.

- To encourage the child or young person to understand trauma, its impact and what can help, supporting them to be more self-aware and to develop a more positive sense of self.

Drawing from experience of how the expressive arts helped her personally, and in her therapeutic work with children and young people with a trauma history, Juliette provides both the knowledge and practical tools to work creatively and safely with trauma.

Introduction

Trauma often lies beyond words. For many, words do not do justice to our internal experiences. So how do we begin to open the Pandora's Box that a child with trauma brings to us – let alone find the 'hope' that is also hiding there in the darkness? One effective way, is for trusted adults to provide a safe environment for children to use another kind of language – a second language of creative, non-verbal, or symbolic expression.

Giving a child an opportunity to work with the creative metaphors and symbols of a story such as *The Silent Selkie* allows them to remain at a safe distance from the source of their own emotional pain, whilst also offering a supportive way for them to communicate that which may be unspeakable.

This expression can give rise to a deep sense of release and relief in children and young people, especially when the adult witnessing their story can convey empathy and emotionally resonate with their childhood wounds. Through the arts, the young person may begin to differentiate their true self from what happened to them – which is a vital step on the road to recovery.

The symbolism contained within the story *The Silent Selkie* and the accessible contents of the guide, make this an ideal tool for adults working with children who have experienced trauma, such as SENDCos, teachers, teaching assistants and family support workers.

However, healing from trauma is a complex process that takes time.

Using this guide may be a first step on a young person's journey towards healing. It may be a path that runs alongside more formal, specialist therapy and long-term support for a young person, or part of a much bigger picture or plan for the young person.

How to use the guide

The first part of the guide is for the adult 'helper' to read. It explains a bit about trauma, its impact and what adults can do to help. It is important to read this section of the guide carefully before beginning any therapeutic work. The second part of the guide is an expressive arts workbook for the child or young person to explore with the helper, alongside the story *The Silent Selkie*.

Ten exercises are provided in Part 2 to encourage healthy creative expression and to help the child or young person to understand trauma, its impact and what can help. The exercises are ordered in a certain sequence to begin with safety-promoting activities and lead up to deeper work on managing emotional experiences. Strengths-based activities are included towards the end to build up the child's self-esteem and resilience before they finish the programme.

The exercises are meant to be completed in small steps, perhaps weekly, with a trusted adult. They are not designed to be exhaustive but a guide to the kinds of activities that might be useful, given the rich symbolism of the story (see the glossary at the end of the Guide).

However, all activities are optional, and their use will depend on the adult's knowledge of the child. For example, it is not advisable to use these exercises with children or young people who are currently suffering too much to be able to access a creative curriculum.

To ensure safety, there is usually a choice to stay within the metaphor of the story, or to carry out more personal work. Children will typically work at the level they feel comfortable with. However, if necessary, provide increased safety by reducing demands and using the arts in a more non-direct way (i.e. being child-led).

This programme is designed to be used with children and young people, however, it may also be used creatively with young or older adults alike, as part of a creative arts project around trauma. Activities can be carried out either 1:1 with an individual pupil or in a circle with a small group, depending on the children you are working with. If working in a small group, you might like to incorporate other nurturing activities into the circle such as a feelings check-in, food sharing and mindfulness exercises.

Part 1

For the helper

About trauma: the psychological wound

Emotional and psychological trauma is the result of adverse events that threaten a child's sense of safety and security, making them feel frightened or overwhelmed, as well as helpless, powerless, and isolated.

Trauma has been described as occurring

> from an event, series of events, or set of circumstances that is experienced by an individual as physically or emotionally harmful or life threatening and that has lasting adverse effects on the individual's functioning and mental, physical, social, emotional, or spiritual well-being.

(SAMHSA, 2014)

This definition highlights the '3Es of trauma' according to SAMHSA (2014): a particular **event** may be **experienced** as traumatic for one individual and not for another, leading to differing **effects** in terms of the long-term impact.

Emotional and psychological trauma can be caused by any adverse event(s) that disrupts feelings of safety and security, for example:

- **One-off events,** such as an accident, injury, or attack. Or other overlooked causes such as the sudden death of a loved one, the breakup of a significant relationship, surgery in infancy, or an experience that felt deeply disappointing, especially if someone acted in a way that was inhumane or deliberately cruel.

- **Ongoing, cumulative stress,** such as adverse events that occur repeatedly, e.g. abuse, neglect, domestic violence, an unstable or unsafe environment, separation from a parent, bullying or discrimination, or other environmental adversities such as poverty, poor housing conditions, having to flee your home and war.

If an external adverse event is the 'arrow', trauma is akin to the 'wound'. But this is a hidden **psychological or emotional wound**, rather than a physical wound.

Trauma is therefore what we experience *internally*, rather than the event itself.

'Developmental', 'complex' or 'relational' trauma is the term used to describe the impact of repeated adverse childhood experiences (ACEs) such as abuse, neglect or violence, within the important relationships of a child's (early) life.

The more frightened, helpless and isolated a child feels, the more likely they are to experience an event as traumatic.

It has been said that adversity turns into trauma when we experience our mind as being alone (Fonagy, 2019), when we do not feel seen or heard, when we have no-one to turn to in our distress.

Research also suggests that there is an increased likelihood that an event may be experienced as traumatic by children already under significant stress, who have suffered a series of losses, or who have been traumatised before.

However, with the support of a trusted adult, it is possible to take small steps to process what has happened, learn to trust and connect with others again, and regain a strong sense of self.

Main difficulties associated with the impact of trauma

Trauma is a source of **intense emotional pain and suffering**, which can lead to a range of debilitating difficulties.

Self-esteem and self-worth

The hidden psychological wound of trauma causes a loss of connection to the 'Self', which can result in very low self-esteem and self-worth. The child may have a tendency to 'abandon' themselves and revert back to early defence mechanisms or survival identities ('false-selves') that were created when faced with stress. Fuelled by 'toxic shame', the child may have distorted thinking patterns – they may be highly self-critical or have limiting beliefs about themselves. In addition, they may feel as if they are damaged, broken or missing something. As a result, they may try to feed the wound or plug the gap with unhealthy external addictions or attachments, rather than connecting in a more healthy, creative way with the source of self-love needed to heal from within.

Attachment development and social relationships

A child with a background of trauma may have developed insecure attachment strategies or survival identities that affect how they relate to others. When a child tries to protect themselves from feeling emotional pain, this can prevent anyone else from connecting with them authentically. The child may be highly distrustful and socially anxious, missing out on experiences that enrich their lives, including social relationships. Or they may be over-trusting and struggle to set boundaries. Living in a way that allows space for social relationships means that we must slowly let go of any protective layers that we have developed to cope with feelings of vulnerability. This comes through building trust and a sense of security.

Curiosity, learning and growth

A child who has experienced trauma may have developed narrow or inflexible thinking patterns in order to protect themselves. This can impact on their capacity to be curious, to learn and to grow. It is important to acknowledge and feel pain – to be brave enough to allow ourselves to face it – and, if possible, to name the pain in order to heal it. If we protect our wound defensively or neurotically pick away at it, rather than opening ourselves up to healing, we may also keep all that is strong and powerful locked inside. Our wound does not define us or dictate our life story – it is only one part of our whole.

Dissociation

Another symptom of trauma is dissociation, where a child escapes from the reality of the present moment into their mind in order to cope. Children who have experienced emotional pain may dissociate more easily in everyday situations, much like entering a trance-like state.

There are different kinds of dissociation but two that are often cited are depersonalisation (feeling disconnected or detached from oneself) and derealisation (feeling disconnected from one's surroundings).

Memory

Memories of traumatic events are often fragmented memories – rather than linear or chronological. This can make it difficult for a child to process what has happened to them. They remember memories as a jumble of confusing feelings or snatches of sensory impressions that are hard to convey using words alone. Following periods of dissociative amnesia, children who have experienced painful adverse events, may 'awaken' as if from a dream to remember the nightmare of their past with memory flashbacks, which can be both terrifying and disorientating. As if a spell is suddenly broken, the person's identity can disappear as if in a puff of smoke and be eclipsed by another identity altogether, as they try to reconcile the memories of their past with their present state.

Sensory processing needs and hypervigilance

In addition to this, the wound of trauma can affect how children manage perceptions, resulting in hyperarousal and sensory processing difficulties. Children may be hypervigilant to their environment and only pay attention to what is deemed necessary for survival, therefore missing other important cues or information that impact on their ability to live life to the full.

Individuals with trauma may also suffer with chronic tension or joint pain due to 'body armouring' (or other physical manifestations of 'toxic stress').

Hypersensitivity and emotional reactivity

Children with trauma may have difficulties with emotional regulation, becoming easily dysregulated. Research shows that traumatic events can cause a repeated activation of a child's biological stress response system (or amygdala) (Perry and Szalavitz, 2006), disrupting healthy emotional processing.

The result of this over-activation is hypersensitivity and emotional reactivity: the child is sensitised to feelings of stress throughout life (Phillips and Shonkoff, 2000) and may have hair-trigger emotional reactions – known as 'emotional flashbacks' (Walker, 2013) – to seemingly small (or imagined) stresses or threats.

Behavioural responses

Children who have experienced trauma may develop rigid behavioural responses rooted in intense (yet often unconscious) fear, in order to protect themselves from feeling more emotional pain than they feel they can bear.

Behavioural responses are usually related to one (or more) of four main fear-based stress responses (Walker, 2013): Fight, Flight, Freeze and Fawn. Responses such as 'Flop', 'Flock' or 'Appease' have also been noted. Behaviours associated with each of the 4F stress responses are described below.

Fight Controlling, manipulative, aggressive, domineering, critical, selfish

Flight Anxious, hyperactive, obsessive-compulsive, perfectionist, escapist

Freeze Detached, avoidant, guarded, closed off, uncaring, depressed

Fawn People-pleasing, overly-compliant, joker/class clown, performer, easily led, vulnerable socially

It is important to emphasise that these responses are **normal reactions to stress**. They are not permanent pathological traits, but a **response to suffering**, and can be reduced or lessened when a child or young person **feels safe enough to be themselves**.

As such, a child or young person with a background of trauma is not fundamentally flawed. Rather they have temporary and malleable habits that they require support to change - just like we all do.

The impact of trauma: hypersensitivity and the 'false self'

A child or young person who is emotionally reactive and easily triggered to feel upset, is often harbouring an **acute hypersensitivity** to their environment. In children with a background of adverse childhood experiences, this is due to the hidden wound of trauma.

A child or young person may create a defensive 'armour' or 'mask' to protect their wound because they have not felt safe enough to be vulnerable – to be themselves.

The creation of this 'false self' is **an adaptive response to suffering**, rooted in fear (rather than in simply 'being' (Tolle, 2020)). It is a protective, **survival identity** that has developed because there is a deep-seated fear that 'being oneself' is not safe and may result in more hurt.

Tolle (2020) explains this as being like a 'branch cut off from the vine'. But at the root of these false identities lies the child's deeper, truer 'authentic self' – an inner child that requires nurturing and a wound that needs acknowledging and healing.

Young people may become hardened and hold back all that they really are inside, or cut themselves off from their feelings, numbing themselves with addictive behaviours, to protect or soothe themselves from the pain of their wound. In short, they abandon their *true self* in order to survive.

In order to let go of unhelpful or unhealthy habits that we have become attached to, rather than trying to stop the habit (e.g. anger, judgement etc.), we must let go of the part of our (false) self that has formed the unhealthy attachment in the first place. It's a bit like shedding layers to find our true nature – who we really are – inside.

In Jungian psychology this is referred to as the alignment of the Ego-Self axis. In order to pivot back to the self and live more authentically, we need to surrender or dissolve the ego-led personas or false selves and find new ways to adapt to the world. Stein says: "It is the dissolution of the misconstrued persona that is often the first step toward individuation" (Stein, 1982 in Turner, 2005).

However, it can be very difficult and painful to let go of old adaptive coping mechanisms that we have developed to protect our soft underbelly of vulnerability from hurt. It can even be difficult to let go of the pain of a wound, if we have become accustomed to that being part of our identity. Eckhart Tolle calls this the 'pain-body' (Tolle, 2020).

We may think 'If I let go of my protective armour, who will hold me? How will I hold myself? I will be too soft, too small, too weak, too powerless. I will be vulnerable to attack, too exposed – easy prey, easy pickings. I will be hurt. And I cannot allow myself to be hurt again'.

But, to live a rich, authentic and meaningful life, it is vital to keep practising liberating ourselves from behaviours that do not serve us anymore, and to heal the inner wound that we are trying to protect.

To do this, we have to learn to *hold ourselves together* with self-compassion and tenderness. We are learning to let go of a lifetime of armoured layers. It will take time to allow a new, more pliable, protective skin to grow in its place. This growth involves cultivating our self-worth and self-esteem by focusing on the parts of us that we would like to develop – like strengths, talents and capabilities.

To this end, it can really help to have a trusted adult around us who can offer us nurture, compassion, kindness, support, and acceptance, thereby guiding us to show more loving-kindness and compassion towards ourselves.

The role of the trusted 'safe' adult

Many children and young people struggle in school because they do not have experience of a secure base or safe haven to return to when life becomes unsettling, stressful or scary. Without a secure attachment figure to regulate their stress or distress, they live life in a state of fear and develop adaptive fear-based strategies or identities in order to survive.

Unmet emotional needs such as safety, security, or being seen and soothed (Siegel and Bryson, 2020), can incubate immense feelings of fear, distress and rage in young people, which, when left unexpressed, can impact upon their mental health, and on the way they relate to themselves and others.

If the child or young person is hypersensitive due to trauma, they require a patient, empathetic witness – a trusted 'safe' adult – who can support them to feel safe enough to be themselves, so that **the need for survival strategies is reduced**.

Bruce Perry has said: "The best predictor of current functioning in youth is current relational health, not history of adversity" (Perry, 2020: 149).

Resilience research has shown that one of the best ways we can support vulnerable children is to improve their access to one or more caring and supportive adults in their environment (Werner and Smith, 1982; 1992; 2001).

The influential work of Louise Michelle Bombèr (2007; 2020) has been pivotal in highlighting the importance of providing vulnerable children with an additional attachment figure – or key trusted adult(s) in school.

Siegel and Bryson (2020) describe how it is helpful for trusted adults to consider **The Four Ss** when supporting a child. When children feel safe, seen (being known and understood), and soothed (being helped to feel calm again), they develop security (where the child expects that someone is available to meet their needs physically and emotionally). This can help a child to cope better with stress, without resorting to reactive behavioural responses.

One of the main ways we can help a child to feel 'safe' is by using what are known as 'safety cues' – body language and gestures that convey safety and care (Porges, 2017). Linked to this, the approach 'P.A.C.E' ('Playfulness, Acceptance, Curiosity and Empathy' (Hughes and Bombèr, 2013)) is also a valuable way to help build feelings of safety and trust in children who may be mistrustful of their environment.

An effective way to ensure that a child feels 'seen' is simply to attune to the child. Attunement has been described as the capacity to notice what might be going on at any given moment in the mind and body of a child (Bombèr, 2020). This might include the trusted adult paying attention, looking interested, being warm and friendly, listening empathically or giving the child time and space (Kennedy et al., 2011; Education Scotland, 2019). Attuned interactions build a vital connection with the child and allow them to feel nurtured and supported, rather than isolated.

When supporting a child to feel 'soothed', it can be helpful for trusted adults to use an approach known as 'Emotion Coaching' (Gottman and DeClaire, 1998; Gus and Meldrum-Carter, 2016). Emotion Coaching aims to acknowledge low levels of emotion early on and to empathise with, label and validate those emotions as they occur – a process known as 'co-regulation'.

Finally, to enhance feelings of 'security', the **Circles of Security** approach encourages caregivers to aim to be 'bigger, stronger, wiser and kind' – being both a 'secure base' from which their child can explore, *and* a 'safe haven' for their child to return to when they feel stressed (Hoffman et al., 2017).

In a school setting, trusted adults can promote the use of 'Nurturing Approaches' across the school (Education Scotland, 2019) within the context trauma-informed and attachment-aware classrooms (Geddes, 2005).

Trusted adults can also help the child or young person to develop an awareness of the root causes of their emotional pain and to understand the role of previous survival strategies, but to acknowledge the need to replace these unhealthy responses, with **new, healthier coping skills**.

This may involve some psychoeducation for the young person – and adults around the young person – on what might be happening inside their brain and why they are so emotionally reactive (e.g. using this resource alongside Aspden, 2016).

Who can be a trusted adult? It is suggested that the trusted adult has some experience of working with vulnerable children in a 'helping' capacity (e.g. as an emotional literacy support assistant, learning mentor, therapist or counsellor), and has had some training in trauma informed and nurturing approaches. Professional supervision and emotional support for the helper is also recommended.

When to seek further help? If the child's symptoms worsen or persist then more specialist 'trauma-specific' support from a qualified therapist or mental health practitioner may be required.

Emotional reactivity and emotional flashbacks

When we feel triggered by an event or situation, it can feel like an emotional tripwire has been detonated. Our stress response system (the 'amygdala') hijacks our thinking mind by misfiring. This can convince our body to believe we are in extreme danger, prompting us to fight, take flight, freeze or fawn (Walker 2005; 2013).

This strong emotional reaction to a relatively minor stressor is sometimes known as an 'emotional flashback' (Walker, 2013). This is not the same as a 'typical flashback' of a memory, where something we see, hear, feel, taste or smell might trigger a memory of a past trauma causing us to re-live that experience in the present. An 'emotional flashback' is when we feel 'taken over' by deep-seated emotions from the past in the present moment. These intense feelings may be triggered by something that unconsciously takes us back to that past experience, such as a feeling of being scared, trapped or powerless, with no options for escape. However, because there is usually no conscious visual component to an emotional flashback, it may not be identified as a post-trauma response (Walker, 2005).

An intense emotional reaction to a present-day situation might be rooted in feelings we felt in the past during a traumatic event and had to suppress at the time, or they might be feelings about an adverse or traumatic event that has not been fully processed. Emotions typically experienced during an emotional flashback are associated with fear and despair – or manifestations of these feelings such as rage or sorrow (Walker, 2005).

Even when we have been made to feel safe after a triggering event, it can take hours or days (even weeks) for the stress levels in our body to slowly reduce and to feel more like ourselves again after an 'emotional flashback'. Whilst it might feel to those around us that they are being attacked or that we do not want them near, underneath there is a desperate need to feel safe, loved and cared for. However, a lack of trust in others because of current (but past trauma) feelings presents a barrier to reaching out and asking for help (Walker, 2005).

Many adults now realise that isolating, punishing, or even trying to reason with a dysregulated child – rather than regulating them – really just shifts them from one survival state to another – one stress response to the next – it does not move them to a place of calm.

To effectively support a child who is emotionally reactive, it is helpful to have a **Safety Plan** of what can help the child to feel regulated (see Exercise 6). It is also beneficial to cultivate a **Daily Self-Care Practice** (see Exercise 10).

Whereas the Safety Plan is a short-term action plan to cope with a triggering event, a Daily Self-Care Practice is a long-term 'prescription' that slowly acts on the nervous system to gradually increase resilience to stress.

If emotional reactivity and dysregulation is caused by a repeated activation of the child's *stress response system (the sympathetic nervous system)*, then in order to counteract this and create a more balanced nervous system, we need to repeatedly focus our attention on activating the child's *relaxation response system (the parasympathetic nervous system)* to help them to feel regulated.

Whilst stress responses cause us to *contract in fear*, self-care practices such as breathing, meditation, yoga or time in nature, provide us with opportunities to *open up* and *allow space for relaxation, restoration and renewal*. Slowly, over time, with daily practices of self-care, the frequency, duration and intensity of emotional flashbacks can lessen.

Just the act of 'showing up for yourself' through a daily self-care practice can create positive changes for a young person. It can help them to cultivate a healthier relationship with themselves.

Through self-care practices, we learn to re-balance ourselves:

Care for the self (rather than fight)

Ground the self (rather than take flight)

Soften the self (rather than freeze)

Honour the self (rather than fawn)

Every day, we can hold onto hope for a young person and encourage them into opportunities to take steps to form **new habits and neural pathways** – not alone, but supported – whether by friends and community, or safe people and places.

Healing from trauma: tending to the roots

Peter Levine has said that "Some things must be dealt with at the roots. Trauma is one of these things" (Levine, 1997). Painful events can bury deep into a child's psyche so that **the behaviours we see expressed are symptoms of the wound of trauma**.

But, when working with a child, we may never know the source of the original 'arrow' or adverse childhood event. We may not even realise a trauma wound is there at all. Often, all we see are the dysfunctional behaviours that manifest in the child as a result; however, if we are not trauma informed these behaviours may not be recognised as originating from an adverse childhood experience.

This hidden residue of trauma can therefore be misconstrued or misinterpreted by adults around a young person. A child's actions are frequently viewed through a myopic 'behaviourist' lens that only deals with the observable behaviours, rather than understood in the wider human context as a distorted communication of an underlying, unmet need – an emotional pain – that is hidden from view.

As adults, we need to be aware of what unmet emotional needs a child's outward behaviour is communicating so that we can help a child to heal from their trauma, rather than simply trying to control or change their symptoms.

When we see an iceberg coming towards us, it is not the tip that we should be concerned about, but what lies beneath. Equally, what lies beneath a child's behaviour is where the focus of our attention and care needs to be.

Simply, trying to extinguish the unwanted behaviour will not make 'behaviour' go away. While fear remains, while the emotions underneath the behaviour remain suppressed, the behaviour just shapeshifts into something else – and that something else could be something far more insidious than the original behaviour – like addictions, mental health issues, ill health or crime.

Rage: the shadow side of unspeakable pain

Rage is often viewed critically, rather than through a lens of compassion and empathy for what caused it. However, anger and rage are as normal and natural as any other emotion, especially if we feel that one of our values or boundaries has been violated. In fact, rage has been described as the 'shadow side of unspeakable pain' (Leavy, 2020).

Whilst we may want a child to show only 'positive' emotions, if we are dismissive, disapproving or ignoring of a child who shows anger, worse still, if a child is made to feel shame for their anger, this can dehumanise the child, which only fuels the fire of self-loathing, adding to the suppression of feelings – rather than their healthy expression.

As adults around a child or young person, it is vital that we recognise the emotion of anger or rage in a child as an opportunity to connect with them, and, not only show empathy, but also validate this emotion – and understand its source. Only then will the child really feel seen and heard.

This **provides a safe space for the child to address other strong emotions or experiences that might be behind the rage**, such as grief, sadness, and emotional abandonment.

Recovery from trauma is a gradual process. It often feels like navigating a 'snakes and ladders' board. We might have days or weeks characterised by tremendous upward growth, then an emotional flashback can cause us to plunge backwards, which can feel like we are having to start all over again.

Because of this, it is important not to shame the child for having an emotional flashback. Shame can result in an even greater downward spiral and a sense of despair that can have very negative consequences. Instead, to promote their long-term resilience, it is essential to provide the child with a sense of hope.

Encourage the child to keep growing by practising their coping tools and reassure them that in time it will be okay.

Whole school approaches: the conditions for growth

A child with a background of trauma will require a caring and nurturing school environment that is child-centred, trauma informed, and attachment focused, and in which they are viewed in the context of their unique humanity. The following *pedagogical stances* are suggested for any trauma informed approaches used in schools:

The conditions for growth

- Developmentally sensitive: informed by the developmental needs of the child and evidence of what environmental features nurture healthy child development, rather than pathological paradigms (i.e. what has gone wrong in the child's brain).

- Strengths-based: implemented through the lens of critical hope and resilience, where children are recognised for their strengths, talents and interests, as opposed to their deficits, disabilities or disorders.

- Relational: concerned with valuing, nurturing and restoring positive and healthy relationships, especially safe and secure attachments with trusted adults – rather than using 'one-off' programmes.

- Eco-systemic: considered against the backdrop of the child or young person's timeline and wider community, including socio-economic, educational, and cultural conditions.

- Ecological: underpinned by a whole-school and community ethos of safety and care, where everyone acknowledges the part they play in a child's wellbeing and resilience to adversity.

- Each of these five foundational stances provide the fertile conditions for therapeutic interventions to be more effective, thereby ensuring that we enable, rather than disable **a child's innate resiliency potential** (Ttofa, 2021).

For further information about key protective factors, strategies and approaches that can enable a child's resilience within a school setting, a 'Nurturing Resilience Card Deck' has been created that may be a helpful accompaniment to this guide for the school as a whole (Ttofa, 2020).

Using the expressive arts with a child or young person who has experienced trauma

One of the ways in which a trusted adult can encourage a child to connect with their deeper, truer authentic 'inner self' and express their hidden childhood wounds safely is by using the expressive arts. Rumi is famous for saying that "The wound is the place where the Light enters you." Similarly, in the podcast 'Stories to Save Us', Michael Meade (2020) has said that knowing one's wound is essential to becoming a human being – an awakened person. In other words, adversity or trauma can be a starting point to a 'rite of passage' that leads to growth, if we are guided by mentors or trusted adults, who can offer the required support.

Stories and the expressive arts have been used since the beginning of time to help human beings to cope with the human condition. Using our imagination alongside mark making can help us to create order and make sense of the often chaotic world around us. It can also aid us in describing and communicating our complex inner world.

Expressive arts might include art and crafts, music, drama, storytelling, sandtray work, writing or dance. Simply allowing the child or young person to draw or make something each week, while you build a relationship with them and talk (if the child wants to) – in a creative space – may be therapeutic for the child. This is not 'therapy' but using the arts in a way that may be positive to the child's wellbeing. However, being creative and using the expressive arts is something that any one of us can do because it is so natural to the human condition. Some might argue that creativity is in fact our natural state of being (Cameron, 1992).

Offering a range of play-based or expressive arts activities for a young person to choose (depending on their age or stage of development), in a *non-directive* manner, can be a helpful way to support a child during periods of adversity. Allowing the child or young person to lead on what they do will support them in their creative expression. More *directive creative approaches*, such as those within part two of this guide, can facilitate both the expression and the containment of emotions associated with traumatic experiences, which may be too painful for the young person to talk about.

Differences between therapy and using the arts therapeutically

Therapeutic work and mentoring generally tend to work with what is already known, not with the depths of the unconscious mind (Thierry, 2017).

Drawing on an analogy, using the arts in a therapeutic way might be akin to us taking a short walk with a friend through a forest, using nature to support our feelings of wellbeing as we stop to notice the birds singing, breathe in the fresh air or feel the warmth of the sun on our faces. What we need as we walk is a trusted person to accompany us, and to share and witness what we see and feel. This is in contrast to finding a naturalist to support us on a much longer walk through much darker, thicker undergrowth; a guide who, through their own training and experience of walking in the forest, understands the significance of some of the paths we are walking to our overall journey towards healing.

In the first example (using the arts therapeutically), our intention is for the child to work with what is *conscious* in order to achieve a general sense of *increased happiness and wellbeing, whilst we follow a set of trauma informed principles*. In the second example (specialist therapy), the person working with the child has a healing role. This requires them, for example, to understand the processes and mechanisms of the psyche, as well as the significance of symbolic representation, having explored their own 'inner world' in training. Our intention in this second scenario is for the child to *heal from the unconscious wounds of trauma using a trauma-specific therapy*.

In both cases, the child is leading the way and we follow. There is no agenda, target or specific route we are following on a map. We are guided by the inner inclinations of the child and what they wish to express. However, as subtle as the difference between the two approaches may be, the second approach requires extensive specialist training and careful supervision from an experienced supervisor.

Despite this distinction, there is often a blurring between therapy and therapeutic work. For this reason, this guide provides some key elements to consider when using the expressive arts as therapy or therapeutically in relation to trauma.

'The therapeutic triangle'

There are three key inter-related elements to consider before undertaking any expressive arts work with a child or young person with a background of trauma. These are:

1. **The safe space**

2. **The trusted adult**

3. **The creative materials**

Each inter-related element of the therapeutic triangle reflects the trauma-informed sequence of engagement: Regulate, then Relate, then Reason (Perry and Ablon, 2019). Like the resounding of a 'triangle' in music, if all three elements of this therapeutic triangle successfully combine, they allow the child's voice to be heard (element four). A fifth element can then be achieved, which is **emotional resonance.** This is the resounding feeling we have in our hearts and minds when we feel we are truly understood.

The child or young person's voice is central to the other three elements and we should always *be guided by their safety*. Every effort should be made to get to know the child. We do not need to know or ask the child about the adverse event(s), however, an understanding of the child's story or background via parents or carers, will be important before commencing therapeutic activities with them.

The Safe Space (emotional regulation)

When working with a child with a background of trauma, it is essential to provide a safe and protected, nurturing space so that the young person feels regulated. This is sometimes referred to as the 'Temenos' (Turner, 2005).

This is a bit like a cast for a broken arm or leg. We are putting in place a protected space for the child's own "innate self-righting tendency" (Werner and Smith, 1992: 202) to begin to work. This resiliency mechanism is what will help move a child towards normal development.

It is important to establish clear and consistent boundaries by ensuring the room you are in is free from distractions, having a few rules that you stick to and by creating a sense of routine or 'rhythm' to the session e.g. explaining what will happen, timings, beginnings, endings. Additionally, ensure the child or young person understands procedures around confidentiality and safeguarding.

It is also vital to make sure you are 'trauma informed' before you begin therapeutic work. For example, ensure your approach is informed by SAMHSA's (2014) six principles of a trauma informed approach: *Safety; Trustworthiness and Transparency; Empowerment, Voice and Choice; Collaboration and Mutuality; Peer Support; and Being Respectful of Cultural, Historical, and Gender Issues.*

The most important thing is for you to create for the child or young person a safe psychological space in which to breathe and express themselves. This is the path towards beginning to heal from a deep wound.

Safety is conveyed by our body language and the way we connect with children and young people – these are known as 'safety cues' (Porges, 2017). Non-verbal communication or 'cues' that conveys safety and care can often deepen connection in a subtle yet profound way (Levine, 2010).

As Perry says: "Troubled children are in some kind of pain – and pain makes people irritable, anxious and aggressive. Only patient, loving, consistent care works: there are no short-term miracle cures" (Perry and Szalavitz, 2006: 244).

The trusted adult (therapeutic relationship)

The quality of therapeutic relationship between a child and a trusted adult is the determining factor in the effectiveness of any therapeutic intervention.

Providing an authentic, attachment relationship where the child or young person feels safe, heard, valued and understood by a benevolent 'empathetic witness' comes before any programmatic concerns. As Gabor Maté says: "Trauma is not what happens to us, but what we hold inside in the absence of an empathetic witness" (Gabor Maté in Levine, 2010: xii).

A child needs a nurturing, trusted adult to be present, to notice and observe what they do, and to tune-in to them. It is also important for the trusted adult to deeply listen to anything the child or young person says for the purposes of understanding – not fixing.

Be genuinely curious, offer non-judgemental acceptance, demonstrate unconditional positive regard and use empathic verbal or non-verbal responses. This simple way of attuning to a young person lays the foundation for the growth of a therapeutic relationship that is built upon trust.

This nurturing approach is very different to the kind of approval that might be contingent upon outcomes and attainment often prolific in an educational environment. However, it is through consistent care, kindness, compassion, patience, empathy, nurture and support – the 'golden thread' of human relationships – that a young person can be enabled to begin a healing process.

Bruce Perry (Perry and Szalavitz, 2006: 244–245) has said: "One of the greatest lessons I've learned in my work is the importance of simply taking the time, before doing anything else, to pay attention and listen."

This is not a quick-fix, and can take time, especially when a child or young person has experienced much adversity or hostility in their life. But the value of this approach is immeasurable as it can restore a child's belief in the goodness of humankind – and in their own intrinsic goodness.

The creative materials (recovering the resilient self)

Creativity is natural to human existence and has been used as a way for individuals to express what happened to them, as well as process and reflect on human experiences, for thousands of years.

If we want children to talk about their internal experience of trauma, we must use their language – the language of play, imagination and creativity.

We can use the expressive arts either *directively* (i.e. with adult-led activities) or *non-directively* (i.e. using child-led activities). Which approach we use will depend on the safety of the child or young person, and how much demands they can cope with. If in doubt, pull back to using non-directive approaches.

Creative approaches allow children and young people to begin to express what they may have previously suppressed – consciously or unconsciously. Through the expressive arts, doors that might have been previously closed, may open up and give a rich freedom of expression to a young person's inner world.

Working with the expressive arts allows a young person to explore and express **deeply intimate and painful experiences using the ancient language of symbols, images and metaphors, without having to detail anything personal**. It permits a child to play with, or play out, memories or experiences in a safe way – at their own pace, without being forced or directed to talk about anything they are not ready to.

As a result, the child has the chance **to separate themselves from what happened to them**, which allows them the psychological space to make sense of their experiences. In short, it is the play or the creative materials that facilitate the child's ability to 'talk' about, reflect on and make sense of adverse events, which in turn, supports their healing. James Hillman writes that: "They [the arts] bridge between the child's first world of imagination and the actual world into which it descends, thereby providing a hands-on way of healing" (Hillman, in Allan 1988: xiv).

The arts also form a **helpful channel between a young person and a trusted adult**, so that a positive connection can be reinforced. Keeping the image within a metaphor enables the young person to feel that their experience has an empathetic witness, whilst respecting any defences that they maintain so as to avoid feelings of exposure or vulnerability.

Using the arts can metabolise the energy of emotion into expression or creativity, rather than suppression and destruction. Sometimes referred to as the 'prima materia' (Turner, 2005), the raw materials used in the expressive arts such as ink, charcoal, pastel pigments, paints, crayons and clay, are often derived from the earth or our natural environment. They are sensory-rich – visual, kinaesthetic, tactile, auditory, olfactory and affective – which not only aids mark-making but also supports the expression of deep, visceral emotions.

For example, it is one thing to describe the feeling of anxiety verbally with words, but it is something much more powerful when we can paint it using a metaphor as a vermillion red octopus growing and swirling amongst churning charcoal waves. We begin to feel what that is like in our bodies, rather than just think it with our mind. For this reason, many find that using raw, natural art materials creatively is hugely therapeutic.

Because of their natural, sensory properties, **art materials tap into the lower parts of the brain** and can therefore provide a vital channel for the strong, physical and sensory energy of big emotions associated with trauma.

To change behavioural states, it is necessary to reach the nervous system and the body, which is connected to our brain. Traumatic memories are not usually encoded as normal explicit or narrative memories in the 'upper brain' or neo-cortex. They are encoded as implicit memories, that include feelings and sensations, in the 'lower brain' – the limbic brain and brain stem. Therefore, children need to access these less conscious areas of the brain in order to process difficult, or unconscious, memories or feelings.

Cognitive approaches that deal with thoughts or words alone, may not fully mobilise the energy of powerful emotions within the body and nervous system – something which Peter Levine (2010) refers to as 'the unspoken voice' of the body. Words, therefore, may fall short when it comes to helping a young person to make sense of their experiences – using all of their senses.

The expressive arts and creative activities provide a conduit between the lower and upper parts of our brain, as well as encouraging whole brain-body integration. This can then help the young person to discover or happen upon solutions to any problems.

Finally, the expressive arts and the natural process of creativity can support a child to express their own authentic and unique personality, separate from their trauma, which can help them to develop a stronger and more positive sense of self. This will also strengthen their self-esteem and contribute to their self-growth, all of which is vital for the development of resilience.

Encouraging a connection to the 'Self' in this way, allows psychological wounds to be tended to, thereby cultivating self-compassion and self-worth, as opposed to more self-destructive or addictive tendencies. Ignoring the wounds of the self may drain a young person of their vital reserves; moreover, it may force a young person to shut off from their pain or seek out other less healthy connections to ease their suffering.

Using the expressive arts, we can help a child or young person to take baby steps towards showing their vulnerability and honouring their sensitivity, until eventually they are able to take off their masks, shed their armour and let go of their defences. In doing so, they discover that underneath the layers, their deeper, truer authentic self has always been there, waiting to shine through.

John Allan concludes:

Healing occurs within this context through relationship both to the therapist and to the expressive media. Much emotion is experienced through action, image and fantasy activities. Problems are expressed, traumas enacted, pain felt, and eventually reparation and transformation occur. The materials – paint, pencil, crayons, toys, sand and clay – are important vehicles facilitating expression, movement and growth, as are the acts of creation, imagination, play and drama. Through these activities a child moves from initial loss, pain and hopelessness to self-control, flexible mastery and humor. The act of 'doing' in the presence of the therapist seems to repair broken images and lead to healing.

(Allan, 1988: xxii)

The child's voice: telling the trauma story

The culmination of providing the child with a safe space, an empathetic witness and relevant creative art materials, is that the child's voice can slowly begin to be heard. It is a huge privilege to hear and see a child's trauma story unfold either through metaphor and image, or in spoken words.

As trusted adults our role is to convey a sense of hope and belief in the child's innate resiliency potential, whilst also honouring a child's vulnerability and respecting their sensitivity by holding space for painful memories to surface slowly and gently. This is a child-led process that must not be forced or directed. We must respect the child's right to talk – or not, and to choose whether – or not – to partake in any therapeutic approach. As Perry says:

> The bottom line is that people's individual needs vary, and no one should be pushed to discuss trauma if they do not wish to do so. If a child is surrounded by sensitive, caring adults, the timing, duration and intensity of small therapeutic moments can be titrated by the child.
>
> (Perry and Szalavitz, 2006: 166)

Levine (1997) writes that before Perseus set out to conquer Medusa, he was warned by Athena not to look directly at the Gorgon as she would turn him to stone. So, Perseus used a shield to reflect Medusa's image and, by doing this, he was able to cut off her head. Such is the case with trauma. If we attempt to confront trauma head on and are too intent on discovering the details of a child's pain, the trauma will continue to do what it has already done – immobilise the child in fear.

The solution to releasing a young person from their prison of isolation and helping them to communicate their pain comes not through confronting trauma directly, but by working with its reflection. In other words, we must take care to work from the expression (or song) of trauma (transmitted to us by means of the expressive arts), slowly towards its source, not the other way around. In this way, the child or young person is not triggered into a state of immobilisation through feeling unsafe, and there is less danger that they will be re-traumatised by the therapeutic process itself.

Van der Kolk warns us: "Truth, like love and sleep, resents Approaches that are too intense" (W.H. Auden in van der Kolk, 2014: 125).

To heal, children do not always need to *talk* about the details of their trauma experience. Communication may come in many forms – words are not the only medium. For many, words are too meagre a tool to use to convey or give meaning to our internal experiences. As the writer Gustave Flaubert wrote:

> For none of us can ever express the exact measure of his needs or his thoughts or his sorrows; and human speech is like a cracked kettle on which we tap crude rhythms for bears to dance to, while we long to make music that will melt the stars.

(Flaubert, 1857: 215–216)

Achieving emotional resonance

Without a trusted adult who *resonates emotionally* with the child's trauma story, the expressions of a child may feel to them like an empty clanging that 'falls on deaf ears'. As the bible says: "If I speak in the tongues of men or of angels, but do not have love, I am only a resounding gong or a clanging cymbal" (New International Bible).

Paul Ekman (2010) has identified that one the key building blocks of empathy and compassion is our ability to achieve 'emotional resonance' with another. Peter Levine echoes this saying:

> as social creatures, it is through empathy that we make our deepest communications. To do this we must be able to "resonate" with the sensations and emotions of others; we must, in other words, be able to feel the same things as those around us feel. The way we indicate this is primarily non-verbal; it is through our postures and expressive emotions.
>
> (Levine, 2010: 42)

When we resonate with another emotionally, we understand that adversity unites us all and we feel this deep within us as a source of empathy and compassion. This can then be communicated back verbally through our language and the way we relate to each other non-verbally.

Joe Tucci has used the analogy of 'whalesong' to describe the growing chorus of trauma knowledge and understanding that is resounding in society at large (cited in Cherry, 2018). This 'whalesong' represents the shared voice of empathy and compassion that echoes far beyond what divides and separates us.

The Eastern Goddess 'Kuan Yin' – the Goddess of Mercy and Compassion – has a thousand arms and eyes in the palms of each of her hands so that she can always see people's distress and reach out to encircle them.

Her name also means 'Hearer of the World's Sounds' because, according to Eastern tradition, when Kuan Yin was about to enter heaven, she could hear the cries of humanity, so she did not enter but returned to earth to help all those who suffer. Kuan Yin offers mercy, healing and compassion, whilst always meeting the true inner needs of the self.

This myth serves as a reminder of the power of being an empathetic witness to another's pain and the importance of empathy and compassion.

"I hear a drum in my soul's ear coming from the depth of the stars."
Rumi

Once you have read Part 1, you are ready to dive in …

Checklists for helpers using the therapeutic triangle

The safe space

1. Use a **'safe and protected' contained space** in which to work.	
2. Add **nurturing elements** to the room – ensure warmth, comfort, natural light etc.	
3. Ensure the room is **low-arousal** and **free from distractions**.	
4. Have a few **clear and consistent boundaries** that you stick to and communicate these clearly to the child in a non-threatening, playful or creative way. (Think of boundaries as shared values such as safety and care for each other, care for the materials etc.)	
5. Reassure the child with a repeated sense of **ritual, routine and rhythm** to each session e.g. meet and greet the young person and ask how their week has been before beginning, then ensure a developmentally appropriate ending to the session.	
6. Explain (and remind where necessary) of **confidentiality and safeguarding** in simple, non-threatening language.	
7. Use **'safety cues'** that communicate to the child know that they are safe (psychologically/socio-emotionally/physically) e.g. a warm, friendly demeanour, open stance, warm facial expression, soft gaze, soothing tone of voice and a light, playful manner.	
8. Ensure you are **trauma informed** in the way you work, using trauma informed principles and respecting the child's own boundaries (values).	
9. **Value the child's work**. Tell the child that you will keep what they create safe after the session and explain how (e.g. by taking a photo of it, keeping it in a special folder or box).	
10. **Honour endings**. At the end, acknowledge the work the child has done using a simple script e.g. *"Well done for today – you have worked hard"*. Let them know that you hold them in mind in between sessions.	

The trusted adult

1. Work to develop an **authentic attachment** with the child based on connection and mutual trust (not control, coercion or confrontation).	
2. Offer a **supportive silence** – be present, calm and still, giving space and time to the child and their needs.	
3. Convey **care and safety** using **gentle**, non-threatening non-verbal communication (see 'safety cues').	
4. Pay **attention** to the child – turning/leaning towards them.	
5. Be **attuned** – tune-in to the child's subtle body language, facial expressions and hand gestures.	
6. Be genuinely **curious** and look interested (rather than inquiring or interrogatory).	
7. Offer **non-judgmental acceptance** (be careful not to be critical of the child's actions or use praise as a judgement of the child).	
8. Communicate **unconditional positive regard** through being emotionally warm, caring, kind and compassionate.	
9. **Listen deeply** to what the child says without adding information (listen to understand, not to fix).	
10. Use **empathic** verbal or non-verbal responses e.g. normalise, validate and label emotions that arise (whilst checking you have understood).	

The creative materials

1. **Warmly receive** all **emotional expression** through the arts or play (say yes to expression!)	
2. **Be strengths-based** – convey a sense of hope and belief in the child's innate resiliency potential and positive growth.	
3. Take the stance that **distress is human and temporary** and that we can learn skills to cope, rather than seeing distress as something that is pathological and permanent.	
4. **Be creative** – provide a variety of art/play materials to encourage emotional expression through the child's language – the language of play, symbols, images, metaphor and storytelling.	
5. **Be child-led** – allow the child to choose what to play with and let them focus on play or exploration without interrupting.	
6. **Be flexible**. Trust that the child knows what they need to do to heal. Bring in other materials, books or stories if the need arises.	
7. **Keep within the metaphor** (unless the child talks about something from their own life) – be very cautious about offering your own analysis, reflections or interpretations.	
8. **Do not ask or direct the child to talk** about their experiences or to explain what they have created.	
9. **Honour the child's vulnerability – be kind**. Be aware that the child will be playing out/ expressing painful memories and experiences through their work.	
10. **Encourage authenticity**. Avoid communicating to the child that an outcome of the session is for them to be happy – rather it is about them expressing themselves (however they feel) and having some special time, just for them.	

Part 2

For the child or young person

Using the expressive arts alongside the *Silent Selkie* Story

Below are ten exercises for exploring the storybook *The Silent Selkie* with a helper.

🎨 This icon shows some expressive arts activities that can be used to expand on some key themes in the story. These activities are designed to encourage healthy creative expression, but they might also help you to develop more self-awareness and a more positive sense of self.

They are meant to be completed in small steps, perhaps weekly, with a trusted adult.

🎨 **Some suggested art materials**

Drawing pencils/pencil crayons/crayons

Acrylic, oil, water colour & finger paints/paint sticks

Oil and soft pastels & charcoal

Air-drying clay, play dough or modelling clay & slime

Felt tips/brush pens/acrylic pens

Collage/craft materials and recycled scraps

Sandtray and miniature figures/items from nature

Dissolving paper and tissue paper

Other useful items

A variety of different paper in a range of sizes, paintbrushes or bits of pieces to paint with, glue, scissors, water, aprons, paper towels, waterproof tablecloths.

Exercise 1: *The Silent Selkie*

Read through the story *The Silent Selkie*, noticing any pictures or images that stand out for you.

🎨 My Art Scape

Using art materials of your choice, create a picture based on the story.

This might be a scene you liked or an image of one of the characters.

What art materials would you like to use (e.g. paints, watercolours, pencil crayons etc)?

Think about the colours you would like to use. Will they be bright or dark? Soft or strong?

Will your picture be of a landscape or of a figure? Or might it include both?

Will you have any words in your picture? What will they say?

If you prefer, use a selection of miniature figures, a sand tray and water to create a scene from the story.

This is a special time for you to use art to create your own scene, whatever that means to you.

My Art Scape

Exercise 2: Golden Scales

In the story *The Silent Selkie*, the Selkie's golden scales are described as her 'golden plated armour'.

She uses her scales to protect herself from being hurt because she feels unsafe and is scared of anyone hurting her hidden wound even more.

When the Selkie goes into 'survival mode', she also flicks her tail like a scorpion.

🎨 My Safety Armour

Draw a picture of how the Selkie protects herself when she feels unsafe.

Or, you might prefer to create a picture of the ways that you protect yourself from being hurt when you feel unsafe.

Do you fight or attack? Do you run, hide or escape into an activity? Do you freeze on the spot? Do you shutdown, or shut people out? Or do you try to fit in and people-please?

Is there an image that comes to mind that you feel like drawing?

Some children find it helps to think of an animal or character that they turn into when they feel unsafe.

Draw your picture on the coat-of-arms-shaped mask.

My Safety Armour

Exercise 3: Whalesong

In the story *The Silent Selkie*, the first whale the Selkie meets connects with her in a very special way – using 'whalesong'. The Selkie then meets a school of humpback whales who help her to feel safe.

🎨 My Safe Harbour

Draw a picture of the Selkie's safe place with the whales.

Or, you might prefer to think about what place helps you to feel safe and draw this.

Maybe you are inspired by the story to create your own a safe harbour, a calm watery seascape or scene.

You might have a different landscape in mind, like some hills, woods, a meadow or a field.

Your safe place might be an imaginary place like an enchanted wood or mystical mountain. It might be a memory of a special place. Or it might be somewhere real like a bedroom or a den.

What is it about what you have drawn that helps you to feel safe?

My Safety Harbour

Exercise 4: The Heart of Weather

In the story *The Silent Selkie*, the Selkie cannot speak out loud using words, but communicates her feelings through the weather. When she feels sad, dark clouds gather. When she feels upset, it begins to rain. When she feels cross, the wind howls like wolves. Though the Selkie behaves in these different ways, this is her behaviour – not who she really is inside. Her behaviour is communicating something that she cannot yet explain or express using words.

***

Talking about **feelings or emotions as weather** can help us to recognise, understand and express how we feel in a creative way.

Emotions are natural and fleeting – just like the changing weather. Being mindful of how emotions come and go – like watching our own inner weather – can help us to feel less stuck when we are experiencing a particularly difficult emotion because we know that eventually it will pass.

We can also try to remember that underneath the weather, the sky is always calm and blue – and we can always find that calm place inside of us.

Weather scales: Think about what weather different kinds of emotions might look like? What might emotions like calm, happy, worry, sadness, loneliness, frustration and anger look like? You can draw your answers if you prefer. You could then create a five-point weather scale e.g.: 1. Feeling happy, 2. Feeling a bit worried 3. Feeling frustrated, 4. Feeling annoyed, 5. Feeling angry. Use this to communicate with adults around you how you are feeling and what you need for each stage.

	1.	2.	3.	4.	5.
I Feel ...					
I Need ...					

🎨 My Feelings Forecast

Pause. Close your eyes. What feeling(s) do you notice in your body? Scan your body for any emotions you notice. Now take a few deep breaths in and out, and then when you are ready, open your eyes. What is your feeling telling you that you need? What might help you right now?

Write about or create a picture of the emotion(s) you are feeling as a kind of weather. Just as there can be more than one weather at any one time, we can feel more than one emotion at any one time – so there might be more than one weather in your picture. Or, you might prefer to use coloured plasticine or play-doh to create an image of how you are feeling.

My Feelings Forecast

Exercise 5: Enraged Beyond all Containment'

In the story *The Silent Selkie*, when the Selkie feels rage, there are big storms of thunder and lightning. The whales that the Selkie meets help her to express her rage in a safe way by singing a whalesong and drumming the sea. They also contain the Selkie's big emotions because they provide a circle of safety around her.

***

An **experience of an extremely strong emotional reaction** like rage or deep sadness can be like being in the middle of a **very strong 'emotional storm'**. It is also known as an **'emotional flashback'**.

When we are in the middle of an 'emotional storm' we may feel as if our whole body has been taken over by the emotion. But we can learn to find a calm centre, so that we do not get swept away by it.

We can use 'RAIN' to help. 'RAIN' stands for:

Recognise what is happening,

Allow the experience to be – just as it is,

Investigate what is happening with interest and care, and

Nurture yourself

(Brach, 2021).

In this last stage, we find ways to step back from the feeling we are experiencing and use kind words or actions to calm ourselves so that we do not become the emotion.

Sometimes talking is not enough to release the energy of the emotions we have in our body. At these times, we might need to do an activity using art, song, music or movement to 'emote' how we feel. Moving our body physically can be a safe way to release our energy so that our body feels calmer. After the art activity below, work with your helper to create some shakers and beaters. For example, fill an empty plastic bottle with some rice, dried beans or pulses. Then put some music on and shake it out! Afterwards, practice some deep breathing or listen to a guided meditation track.

🎨 Rage on a Page

Draw a picture of the Selkie's rage.

Or, you might prefer to think about what rage looks like to you and to draw this.

What image comes to mind?

Is it large or small? Is it hard or soft? Is it hot or cold?

How does it make you feel? Where do you feel that in your body?

Notice the qualities of the energy or sensation in your body (you can refer back to your 'safe harbour' if you begin to feel this too strongly or too quickly).

What do you usually do when you are feeling that way?

What words might you spell out?

Rage on a Page

Exercise 6: A Hidden Wound

In the story *The Silent Selkie*, the Selkie has a splinter causing her pain and is the reason why she behaves the way she does. She is also very sensitive to what others say or do because of her hidden wound.

We never find out the 'terrible story' of how the Selkie got her splinter and how she was hurt. How do you think the Selkie got the splinter? What is the Selkie's terrible story that she remembers in her dreams?

***

Think about whether you have ever had something terrible happen to you that caused you to feel sad, scared, hurt, upset or angry. Perhaps this is something that is too painful or confusing for you to express in words.

Instead of a physical wound, sometimes when terrible things happen to us it leaves a kind of **hidden 'emotional wound'** that others cannot see. Eventually, we might hide or cover up this wound, so no one even realises it's there. We may even forget it's there ourselves. But it may still bother us. This is called **'trauma'**.

Sometimes we can talk about our emotional pain to someone we trust, but at other times we might not know how to express it in words, so using art might help. Remember, when something bad happens to you as a child, it is not your fault. Children have a right to be protected from harm.

For the child or young person

🎨 My Hidden Wound

Using the art materials provided, create an image of the Selkie's terrible story and how she got her hidden wound.

Or, you might wish to draw your own hidden emotional wound - whatever that means to you. Perhaps this is something that made you feel sad, scared, hurt, upset or angry. This can look like anything you want it to. It is something that you may want to return to later.

Think about: When did you first notice this? What would help to make the hurt go away? What is it that you need now?

You don't have to talk about this, but you may want to share this with your helper. Or you may want to talk about it at another time.

My Hidden Wound

Exercise 7: The Mouthpiece

 In the story, the Selkie uses a shell as a mouthpiece so that she can call for help. Eventually, the Selkie is heard by a school of humpback whales who understand that the reason she has been acting in an unkind way is that she has been in a lot of pain for many years.

Finally, the Selkie no longer feels alone but that someone is really listening and understanding how she feels. The giant humpback whales help the Selkie to feel safe so that she no longer needs her golden plated armour to protect her wound.

***

Like the Selkie's physical wound, an emotional wound can cause us to develop '**sore points**' or '**soft spots**' about certain experiences that feel unsafe e.g. when something feels like it has 'hit a nerve' – even when there is **no danger at all**.

This can be a '**stress trigger**' for a kind of automatic but '**false alarm**' to go off inside our body and brain in ways that are not helpful. This false alarm can cause an '**emotional flashback**' or '**emotional storm**', which makes us want to '**fight**', '**run/hide**', or '**freeze**'.

In emergencies like this, it is useful to have an '**SOS Safety Plan**' of what can help – a bit like an anchor for a ship during a storm. **Common triggers for emotional storms** are: feeling rejected or separated from a trusted person; change or something new or unexpected; making a mistake, being corrected or criticised; when we don't feel listened to, heard or understood; pressure or demands to achieve or perform; and feeling threatened or betrayed.

We can try to **be more aware** of when we are triggered – when we feel unsafe, unsupported or unloved. We can also try to show ourselves more love, kindness and compassion. Try not to beat yourself up for having an '**emotional storm**' – it is not your fault. With practice and support, you can learn to calm down more quickly and eventually learn to react less strongly and less often.

🎨 My SOS Safety Plan

Using the art materials provided, you might wish to create a large poster or a small card of your own S.O.S. Plan with your helper. This will describe what you can do in an emergency – when you are feeling very overwhelmed or triggered. Is there something you need, someone you can talk to, something you can do that helps to calm you, or a place you can go?

My SOS Safety Plan

My stress triggers are:
E.g. Too many people around me

Safe: My safe place is:
E.g. Space on my own/the den

Seen: My trusted 'safe' adults are:
E.g. Teaching assistant/mentor

Soothed: My calming activities are:
E.g. A change of activity such as going for a walk outside, listening to music, having a cool drink etc

Secure: Routines and rituals that help me are:
E.g. Completing a rhythmic or repetitive activity like building Lego, doing a puzzle or colouring

---

Based on Siegel and Bryson's 4Ss strategy
- 'safe, soothed, seen and secure' (2020).

Tips for the helper on completing a safety plan

My stress triggers

Help the young person to learn to identify the types of triggers that lead to 'emotional storms'. For example, they may need to avoid unsafe people, places, activities and triggering mental processes. This is not to find-fault in them but to help support them to stay safe. If the child is not yet ready to accept help with regulation, help the young person to feel safe and supported using the first two 'S's of the 4Ss (Siegel & Bryson, 2020).

Safe

Give physical and emotional space. Reassure and communicate safety.

Encourage the young person to identify a safe place to go to. They might wrap themselves up in a blanket, hold a stuffed animal, or lie down. Remind the child of the technique 'RAIN': help them to Recognise that they are in an emotional storm (Brach, 2021; Walker, 2005). Though they might feel in danger, they are safe – this is a 'false alarm'. Use a simple script to help e.g.: "You are safe."

Seen

Maintain a calm presence, be patient.

Help the child to cultivate safe relationships and seek support from a trusted 'safe' adult who can be the calm 'safe harbour' or 'anchor' in the storm. The adult needs to be someone who can eventually provide co-regulation – someone who they can go to for reassurance, comfort and protection when they feel lost and scared.

If the child is ready to accept help with regulation, move onto the next two 'S's.

Soothed

Engage the young person in ways that will help them to become more regulated. Attune non-verbally, listen with acceptance, be curious about underlying emotions, validate emotions and offer empathy. Use distraction and a change of activity. Support the child to use calming activities using their senses (e.g. they might go for a walk or have a sensory box with things to hold, play with, smell, listen to or look at). Focus on slow breathing in and out (longer out-breaths are especially calming) and encourage muscle relaxation through calming music or guided meditation tracks.

Secure

Tell the young person that you are there for them. Feeling safe, seen and soothed helps children to feel emotionally secure. To enhance feelings of 'security', the 'Circles of Security' approach encourages caregivers to aim to be 'bigger, stronger, wiser and kind' (Hoffman et al., 2017). Children also cope better when there is more routine so that life is predictable. Some young people find it helpful to do something simple, structured, repetitive or logical to help them to feel secure like building Lego, colouring, counting, repeating a phrase, singing a song or watching a familiar or favourite TV programme. Others like to physically hold themselves together.

Exercise 8: A Winding Trail of Gold

In the story *The Silent Selkie*, the Selkie picks off her scorching golden scales and casts them out to sea.

It seems as if the Selkie is breaking apart but she is really just getting rid of the old body armour that held her back and caused her to act in rigid ways.

Just as a snake sheds its dead skin, the Selkie is actually letting go of her old **'survival identity'** that she created to cope with her pain and protect herself from being hurt more.

The gold scales that surround the Selkie are no longer who she is anymore. Like a butterfly emerging from a caterpillar cocoon, in order to evolve into something new, she must leave behind her old **'false self'**.

What old behaviours or habits do you think the Selkie is letting go of when she casts her scales out onto the sea?

***

Often **angry feelings** or **aggressive behaviour are caused by negative, critical or judgemental thoughts or feelings** either about others or ourselves. These thoughts and feelings are not who we are – they are like a fuel that feeds the fire.

These kinds of **negative beliefs** are known as **self-limiting beliefs**. They can affect how we can grow and what we can achieve.

To reduce feelings of anger, we can try to starve the fire of its fuel by noticing and then **letting go of our negative, critical or judgemental thoughts or feelings** about ourselves or others and trying to cultivate more acceptance, compassion and feelings of self-worth.

🎨 Leaves on the Stream

Think about some unhelpful self-limiting feelings, thoughts or habits that the Selkie might like to let go of when it casts out its golden scales onto the water.

Or, you might prefer to think of some self-limiting beliefs or habits that you wish to let go of. (It might be helpful to think back to the picture you drew on your armour and the survival mode you go into when you feel unsafe.)

Unhelpful thoughts might be things like 'I'm bad', 'I'm not good enough', 'I'm unlovable', 'I'm not worthy'. Feelings might be things like fear, anger, jealousy, resentment, guilt, shame, regret, insecurity, sadness, anxiety or worry. Habits might be things like judgement, criticism, self-criticism or comparing yourself to others – which might lead to aggression, perfectionism or withdrawal.

Write or draw some negative beliefs/habits onto a piece of (water-soluble) dissolving paper. Then drop the paper like an autumn leaf into a bowl of water and swirl the water around until it eventually disappears.

You can also write beliefs or habits you wish to let go of onto stones to throw into a pool of water. Alternatively, use bubbles to blow away negative thoughts – telling them to 'Go Away!' and watch them pop.

This is a nice activity to do in nature with your helper, if possible. It can be very therapeutic to watch old habits be carried away by the wind or water – rather than fight with them.

Make it a daily practice to work at letting go of ways of being that no longer help you. Each time you go to think a negative thought or to use an unhelpful habit or behaviour, try to remember to pause and let it go. Remind yourself this is not who you are inside – it is your 'false self' trying to take over – and instead be compassionate towards your true self.

Repair

In the story *The Silent Selkie*, when the Selkie's golden scales are cast off into the sea, the gold pieces float back to the other seal-folk who the Selkie harmed with her actions. This is a gesture that allows the Selkie to make up for what happened and repair her relationship with the seal-folk. In return, the seal-folk follow the Selkie's winding trail of gold in order to find her and use some of the gold to make the Selkie a crown. This helps the Selkie to feel that she belongs and that she is supported to cope with her emotions, rather than made to feel different or isolated.

When we have done something that is harmful, it is important to have a chance to repair the harm with everyone who was affected.

There are three key steps to repairing harm:

1. What happened and who was affected?
   Work together with your adult helper to identify the harm caused and all who were impacted by it. Like throwing a rock into a pond, the way we behave can affect a lot of different people.

2. How did what happened affect others?
   Consider the ripple effect of your behaviour. Think deeply about how each person was impacted by what happened. For example, how did they feel about what happened? How do you feel?

3. Create and carry out a plan to repair the harm
   Finally, create a plan to repair the harm with each person affected. The plan doesn't have to be anything complicated; it can be as simple as an apology or giving someone a 'sorry card'. Or it might involve doing something kind to make up for what happened.

Exercise 9: A Shimmering New Skin

In the story, after losing all of her scales, the Selkie is very vulnerable to attack because she does not have any protective skin. During this vulnerable time, a humpback whale visits the Selkie each day and sprays the Selkie's body with salty sea water.

This helps to soothe the Selkie's flesh so that her splinter is eased out and her wound is healed.

Finally, like the transformation of a caterpillar into a colourful butterfly, the Selkie grows a shimmering new skin.

She also has a heart that 'dares to feel', which means that she does not shut herself off from her feelings or push them away through her behaviour – but learns how to express feelings safely.

***

Many children and young people who have endured difficult life events possess strengths that others do not, such as being highly sensitive, empathic, intuitive, creative, compassionate, spiritual, in touch with emotions and having an affinity with nature or animals.

A bit like having a shield, when we know our character strengths, these can become 'protective factors' that help to buffer us from stressful or difficult life experiences - giving us greater resilience.

Consider your own unique, whole personality. Both your character strengths, interests and positive aspects. But also things you would like to improve on. As human beings, we should not strive for perfection, but to be real – because 'real people aren't perfect and perfect people aren't real' (Prince EA, 2018).

Your helper can give you some character strengths cards to look through so you can choose five that describe you best. Choose one strength that you would like to get better at too.

Our character strengths are 'protective factors' that can help us to be resilient to stressful or difficult life experiences.

🎨 My Strengths Shield

Like a snowflake, every mandala is unique. Using the art materials provided, create a colourful mandala of who you are – your unique personality. (Your helper can buy a book with different mandalas to colour in or you can create your own.)

As you shade in the segments of your mandala, think about what each colour represents about you – a character strength that you have – and also the character strengths you would like to develop.

My Strengths Shield

🎨 My Values Compass

To protect ourselves, it is important to have clear and consistent boundaries, rather than shutting ourselves off from others with rigid defences or trying to control others through aggressive behaviour.

We can develop boundaries by being aware of our values and asserting what these are in a calm, considered way.

First, complete your Values Compass by writing down four (or more) values that are important to you. These are your own personal needs or limits. You can use character strengths cards to help you to decide what you value in yourself and others (e.g. care, kindness, honesty etc). Your Values Compass will help keep you on track when you go off course.

Then, practice finishing the starter scripts below. Consider what is okay behaviour (what supports your values) and what is not okay behaviour (what goes against your values).

You can stick this Values Compass onto the back of your mandala. This is your strengths shield to represent who you are – your strong 'self'. Use your new shield to protect you and give you extra resilience when you need it.

Remember, we cannot control whether other people respect our boundaries, but we can make sure we are clear about what is important to us. We can then try to repair any ruptures in relationships (like disagreements or conflicts with others) by referring back to these values or trying to create some shared values together.

My Values Compass

Boundaries Scripts

Value: Care

E.g. *It's okay for you to ... borrow my things*
It's not okay for me if you ... do not return them or do not take care of them

My Boundaries

Value:

It's okay for you to ...
It's not okay for me if you ...

Exercise 10: A Golden Crown

At the end of the story, the whales give the Selkie a golden crown to remind her of her strength and ability to cope. What might help you to cope with stressful events going forward? Here are ten tips for daily self-care:

Ground: Go outside for a walk outside in nature, spend time with animals, visit a special place, or bring nature indoors.

Move: Do something to be physically active like yoga, bouncing on a trampoline, dancing, running or martial arts, to 'get out' of your mind.

Breathe: Do some breathing exercises – breathe in through your nose and out through your mouth. Slow down your out-breath to help your body to relax.

Meditate: Listen to a guided meditation or mindfulness track. Imagine your safe place, if that helps. Use prayer if it is something that helps.

Talk: Use positive self-talk to challenge and let go of any past troubling memories, future worries or fears, or unhelpful thoughts. Remember some of your key strengths and repeat a mantra of self-worth ('*I am strong*', '*I am safe*'). Or talk to a trusted adult or friend.

Create: Write in a journal or feelings diary, draw or craft something, do some painting, sculpt clay, make slime, sing along to music, bake a cake.

Calm: Spend time away from the noise of life – being quiet. Slow down. Be aware of people who might over-stimulate or stress your nervous system e.g. by rushing around or using harsh, loud or critical voices.

Unplug: Reduce screen time or social media use, dim lights, remove clutter.

Nurture: Create a cosy den, wrap up in a soft blanket, hug a hot water bottle or a teddy, take a nap, have something nice to eat or drink, watch something funny or familiar on the TV, listen to a favourite story or piece of music, read a magazine or a good book, pamper yourself with a hand, foot or head massage, have a hot bath, use aromatherapy oils.

Be mindful: Remember to be mindful of what is happening 'now', rather than worrying about something in the future or the past. Do a mindful activity to give the 'monkey' mind a job e.g. colouring, logic puzzles.

🎨 My Coping Crown

What things will you do to help you to cope with your own emotional storms and remain calm when faced with everyday challenges?

Write some positive goals for a daily self-care plan. These are ways you will look after yourself each day so that you feel calm, nurtured and soothed. You can write these onto post-its or onto a small card for yourself as a reminder. Or create your own coping toolkit out of a shoebox.

To reward yourself for completing this programme, decorate a sea-crown in a colour of your choice (an example has been provided but lots are available on the internet to download for free or buy – or design your own!). Decorate your crown using art and craft materials or recycled items.

You can imagine you are wearing this crown so that you always have ways to cope when you feel stressed or upset. Or use it as a reminder to plan something nice to do at the end of a difficult day.

Remember: Emotional storms will happen from time to time and it's okay for our coping crown to fall off at times. When it does, use your 'SOS Plan' to reach out for help.

My Daily Self-Care Plan

1.

2.

3.

You can find some more ideas for self-care here:
www.annafreud.org/on-my-mind/self-care/

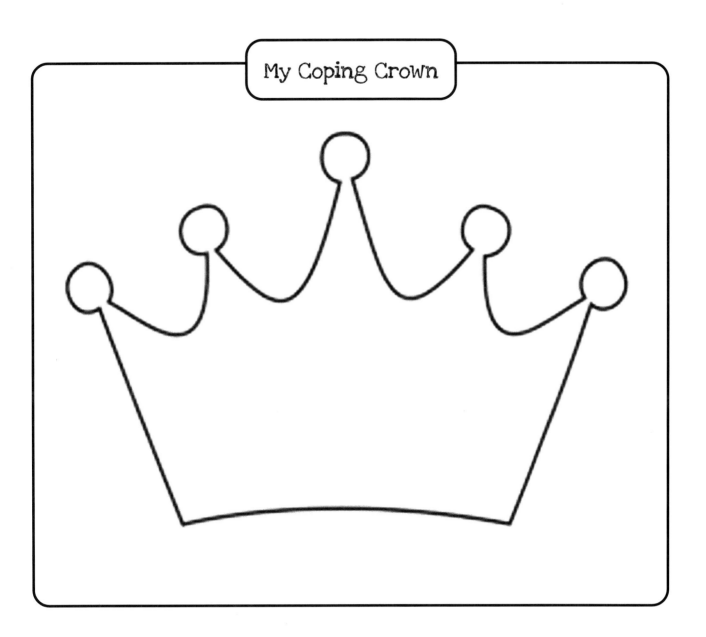

My Coping Crown

Epilogue: Beyond the pain: your story is not over ...

Finally, using the art materials provided, draw a picture of a hopeful 'next chapter' in the Selkie's story. Or you might prefer to write a hopeful poem entitled 'Beyond the Pain' – whatever that means to you – either about the Selkie or about yourself.

Beyond the Pain

Daring to feel: closing mantras

"Many of us spend our whole lives running from feeling with
the mistaken belief that you can not bear the pain.
But you have already born the pain.
*What you have not done is **feel all you are** beyond that pain."*
Gibran, 1923

Who am I beyond the pain?
Beyond the pain I am

....

(Fill in the gap with your own intention or character strength)

Whilst I accept and honour the survival strategies
I developed to cope with my inner emotional pain,
I am working to release these
These are not who I am.

May the wound of my trauma heal
and may I practise caring for my deeper truer self
with kindness and compassion each day.

Author's endnote

Adversarial growth: trauma through a resiliency lens

As a survivor of childhood trauma myself, the overall message of this guide is one of hope in the face of adversity.

Beyond our pain, we are *more* than what happened to us – we are who we become.

Our trauma story is not our only story – and it does not have to be the end of our story.

Healing involves accepting and honouring the defence mechanisms and survival strategies we developed to cope with our emotional pain, whilst working to release these by tending to our deeper, truer self each day. This way, our own sparkling light can shine through.

In order to be whole, we need to embrace our whole self, including our sensitivities and vulnerabilities. Once we learn to honour our hypersensitivity, having a highly sensitive and intuitive side to our personality can be a source of great strength - it is not something to be ashamed of, but rather it is a gift.

As helping adults working with children and young people, it is vital that we convey the sense of hope that change and growth is possible – one small step at a time.

Anne Lamott (1995: 17) says:

> Hope begins in the dark, the stubborn hope that if you just show up and try to do the right thing, the dawn will come. You wait and watch and work: you don't give up.

There are times in all our lives when we may encounter painful experiences and feel as if we have been plunged into darkness.

Rather than this being seen as a symptom of a permanent pathological condition, it may be an essential stage in transformation and growth.

The important thing is that we feel supported to come through this period of change by someone who can nurture our growth, so that we emerge stronger, wiser, and braver.

Juliette

A glossary of the Symbolism in *The Silent Selkie*

Golden scales: The golden scales represent armour and a defended or rigid ego position. They also represent the survival identities that the Selkie has developed to protect herself from further pain, due to her wound, which cause her to act in ways that are not helpful.

Heart of weather: The Selkie's behaviour is communication of a hidden emotional need. She is communicating that she is in pain and that she does not feel heard or seen. The storm is an analogy for an 'emotional flashback' or 'emotional storm'.

Hidden wound: The Selkie's hidden wound is an emotional wound – or trauma – resulting from the impact of an adverse event that was not recognised or processed at the time.

Mouthpiece: The shell mouthpiece the Selkie uses to cry out for help represents her trying to find her authentic 'voice'. It is through the mouthpiece that she connects with the whales, who eventually help the Selkie to feel heard.

Shimmering new skin: The new skin that the Selkie develops at the end, is symbolic of her finding her true self – her true colours. It is a beautiful symbol of transformation that has occurred through a rite of passage that began with a wound.

Singing: When the Selkie sings her song in her dream, this is symbolic of the expressive arts and non-verbal, body-oriented methods of coping with trauma that are indigenous to humankind (Levine, 2010).

Trail of gold: The golden scales that the Selkie casts into the sea are symbolic of how the expressive arts can help us to let go of our 'false self' and recover our true, resilient self. It is also the way the Selkie repairs the harm she has caused to others.

Whalesong: The 'whalesong' is symbolic of the shared voice of human adversity and compassion – the 'resonance' with others' emotions and sensations that Levine (2010) writes about. The drumming of the sea by the whales with their fins is alluding to indigenous collective music and movement circles that are used in healing or celebratory ceremonies.

References

Allan, J. (1988) *Inscapes of the Child's World: Jungian Counselling in Schools and Clinics*. Dallas, TX: Spring Publications.

Aspden, K.L. (2016) *Help! I've Got An Alarm Bell Going Off in My Head!* London: Jessica Kingsley.

Bombèr, L.M. (2007) *Inside I'm Hurting*. Duffield: Worth Publishing.

Bombèr, L.M. (2020) *Know Me to Teach Me: Differentiated Discipline for Those Recovering from Adverse Childhood Experiences*. Duffield: Worth Publishing.

Boxall, M. (2002) *Nurture Groups in School: Principles and Practice*. London: Paul Chapman Publishers

Brach, T. (2021) Resources – RAIN: Recognize, Allow, Investigate, Nurture. www.tarabrach.com/rain/ (accessed 01.04.21).

Burke Harris, N. (2018) *The Deepest Well: Healing the Long-Term Effects of Childhood Adversity*. Bluebird.

Cameron, J. (1992) *The Artist's Way*. Los Angeles: Jeremy P. Tarcher/Perigree.

Cherry, L. (2018) *Day Four – Childhood Trauma Conference*. Cited on www.lisacherry.co.uk (accessed 03.11.2019).

Education Scotland (2019) *Applying Nurture as a Whole School Approach: A Framework to support the Self-evaluation of Nurturing Approaches in Schools and Early Learning and Childcare (ELC) Settings*. Glasgow City Council/Nurturing Glasgow.

https://education.gov.scot/improvement/Documents/inc55ApplyingNurturingAp proaches120617.pdf

Ekman, P. (2010) *The Roots of Empathy and Compassion*. https://greatergood.berkeley.edu/video/item/the_roots_of_compassion (accessed 01.04.21).

Flaubert, G. (1857) *Madame Bovary*, trans. Francis Steegmuller. New York, Random House.

Fonagy, P. (2019, 28 April) 'Therapy saved a refugee child. Fifty years on, he's leading a mental health revolution'. *The Guardian*.

Geddes, H. (2005) *Attachment in the Classroom: The Links Between Children's Early Experience, Emotional Well- Being and Performance in School: A Practical Guide for Schools*. Duffield: Worth Publishing.

Gottman, J. and DeClaire, J. (1998) *Raising an Emotionally Intelligent Child*. New York, NY: Simon & Schuster.

Gus, L. and Meldrum-Carter, L. (2016) *Student Wellbeing: Emotion Coaching in Schools*. www.sec-ed.co.uk

Gibran, K. (1923) *The Prophet*. Black Dog & Leventhal. Illustrated Edition (2020)

Hoffman, K., Cooper, G., and Powell, B. (2017) *Raising a Secure Child: How Circle of Security Parenting Can Help You Nurture Your Child's Attachment, Emotional Resilience, And Freedom to Explore*. London: Guildford.

Hughes, D.A. and Bombèr, L.M. (2013) *Settling Troubled Pupils to Learn: Why Relationships Matter in School*. Duffield: Worth Publishing.

Kennedy, H., Landor, M. and Todd, E. (2011) *Video Interaction Guidance: A relationship-based intervention to promote attunement, empathy and wellbeing*. London: Jessica Kingsley.

Lamott, A. (1995) *Bird by Bird*. New York: Anchor Books.

Leavy, P. (2020) Facebook post (access/dated 31.05.2020).

Levine, P. (1997) *Waking the Tiger: Healing Trauma*. U.S.: North Atlantic Books.

Levine, P. (2010) *In an Unspoken Voice: How the Body Releases Trauma and Restores Goodness*. U.S.: North Atlantic Books.

Lyons, S., Whyte, K., Stephens, R. and Townsend, H. (2020) *Developmental Trauma Close Up*. https://beaconhouse.org.uk/wp-content/uploads/2020/02/Developmental-Trauma-Close-Up-Revised-Jan-2020.pdf

Meade, M. 2020 *Stories to Save Us with Michael Meade* Number 144. Luminary 'Under the Skin with Russell Brand'. Accessed 1 August 2020 via 'Luminary'.

Perry, B. (2020) 'The Neurosequential Model: A developmentally sensitive, neuroscience-informed approach to clinical problem solving' in Mitchell, J., Tucci, J. and Tronick, E. *The Handbook of Therapeutic Care for Children*, pp. 137–158. London: Jessica Kingsley Publishers.

Perry, B. and Ablon, J.S. (2019) 'CPS as a neurodevelopmentally sensitive and trauma informed approach' in Pollastri, A.R., Ablon, J.S. and Hone, M.J.G. *Collaborative Problem Solving in Clinical Psychiatry*, pp. 15–31. Springer International Publishing.

Perry, B. and Szalavitz, M. (2006) *The Boy Who Was Raised as a Dog: And Other Stories from a Child Psychiatrist's Notebook*. New York: Basic Books.

Phillips, D.A. and Shonkoff, J.P. (Eds) (2000) *From Neurons to Neighborhoods: The Science of Early Childhood Development*. Washington: National Academies Press.

Porges, S. (2017) *The Pocket Guide to the Polyvagal Theory: The Transformative Power of Feeling Safe*. W.W. Norton & Company.

Prince, E.A. (2018, 2 July) *Stop Trying to Be Perfect*. YouTube, https://youtu.be/LySC3v5geAc (accessed 26.09.2020).

Siegel, D. and Bryson, T.P. (2020) *The Power of Showing Up: How Parental Presence Shapes Who Our Kids Become and How Their Brains Get Wired*. UK: Scribe.

References

Substance Abuse and Mental Health Services Administration (2014) *SAMHSA's Concept of Trauma and Guidance for a Trauma-Informed Approach*, HHS Publication No. (SMA) 14–4884, Substance Abuse and Mental Health Service Administration, Rockville, MD. https://store.samhsa.gov/system/files/sma14-4884.pdf (accessed 26.09.2020).

Thierry, B. (2017) *The Simple Guide to Trauma: What It Is and How to Help*. London: Jessica Kingsley.

Tolle, E. (2020) *The Power of Now: A Guide to Spiritual Enlightenment*. Yellow Kite Publishing.

Ttofa, J. (2020) *A Nurturing Resilience Card Deck*: *A Resource for Use with Vulnerable Young People*. London: Routledge.

Ttofa, J. (2021) *The Conditions for Growth. Resiliency Enabling Approaches for Children And Young People (REACH) A Guide For Schools In Nurturing The Resilience Of Children With Adverse Childhood Experiences (ACES)*. Sparkle in the Light. www.sparkleinthelight.co.uk

Turner, B.A. (2005) *The Handbook of Sandplay Therapy*. Cloverdale, CA: Temenos Press.

Van der Kolk, B. (2014) *The Body Keeps the Score: Mind, Brain and Body in the Transformation of Trauma*. New York: Penguin Random House.

Walker, P. (2005) 'Flashback Management in Treatment of Complex PTSD'. *The East Bay Therapist*, September/October.

Walker, P. (2013) *Complex PTSD: From Surviving to Thriving*. CreateSpace Independent Publishing Platform.

Werner, E. and Smith, R. (1982) *Vulnerable But Invincible: A Longitudinal Study of Resilient Children and Youth*. New York: Adams, Bannister and Cox.

Werner, E. and Smith, R. (1992) *Overcoming the Odds: High Risk Children From Birth to Adulthood*. New York: Cornell University Press.

Young Minds (2019) *Adversity and Trauma-Informed Practice: A short guide for professionals working on the frontline* by R. Brennan, M. Bush and D. Trickey, with C. Levene and J. Watson.

Useful websites

www.nctsn.org (National Child Traumatic Stress Network)

https://beaconhouse.org.uk

https://touchbase.org.uk/

www.nurtureuk.org/

www.circleofsecurityinternational.com/

www.circle-time.co.uk/our-approach/quality-circle-time/

https://restorativejustice.org.uk/restorative-practice-education-0

www.smilingmind.com.au/

www.headspace.com/

https://yogawithadriene.com/

https://llttf.com/resources/llttf-yp-resources/

www.getselfhelp.co.uk/links2.htm

www.gostrengths.com

https://www.calm.com/

https://innovativeresources.org/resources/card-sets/strength-cards/